ITALIAN
FOOD AND DRINK

Edwina Biucchi

The Bookwright Press
New York · 1987

FOOD AND DRINK

Chinese Food and D
French Food and Dr
Indian Food and Dr
Italian Food and Drink

First published in the
United States in 1987 by
The Bookwright Press
387 Park Avenue South
New York, NY 10016

First published in 1986 by
Wayland (Publishers) Limited
61 Western Road, Hove
East Sussex BN3 1JD, England

© Copyright 1986 Wayland (Publishers) Limited

Library of Congress Catolog Card Number:
86–71546
ISBN 0–531–18120–0

Typeset by DP Press, Sevenoaks, England
Printed in Italy by G. Canale & C.S.p.A., Turin

The author would like to acknowledge
the help of the Italian State Tourist Office,
Piccadilly, London.

Cover Campo dei Fiori market in Rome.

Contents

Italy and its people

The Republic of Italy is a peninsula shaped like a boot or a wrinkled sock, situated between the Adriatic and Tyrrhenian seas in the middle of the Mediterranean. On its northern borders are France, Switzerland, Austria and Yugoslavia. It is 301,225 sq km (116,303 square miles) in area and the population is 57,942,000. The capital of Italy is Rome, which is also the home of the Pope, leader of the Catholic Church. He lives in a separate state within Rome known as the Vatican City.

Central Italy was occupied from about 1000 B.C. by Etruscan, Latin, Sabine and other tribes. Under the Roman emperors, starting with Augustus, who was emperor when Christ was born, Rome gradually grew into a very powerful city so that by 133 B.C. she was already in control of the whole of Italy, Corsica, Sardinia, Spain, Greece and what is now Eastern Turkey.

In the fifth century A.D. Rome was defeated by the Ostrogoths invading from the north and the Byzantines from the south. For the next 1300 years or so, Italy was made up of separate kingdoms and city states and it was not until 1860 that it was finally made into one country. In 1939 at the start of World War II, Italy was on the side of Germany under the Fascist dictator, Benito Mussolini, but then joined Britain and America in 1943 and declared war on Germany. After the war, Italy became a republic. It is now divided into twenty regions and ninety-five provinces, (see map), and is a member of the European Economic Community (EEC).

Today, agriculture is very important to Italy, and there are thousands of small peasant holdings, especially in the poorer south.

Fruit, wines, cheeses and vegetables are important exports, and so too are stylish automobiles, furniture, leather shoes and handbags, plastics and chemicals.

Italy is a very beautiful country with all kinds of different scenery. In the north are snow-covered Alps, the bare Po plain, the barren Apennine hills and the lush and fertile regions of Tuscany and Umbria. Farther south the landscape and climate becomes more "Mediterranean," with hot summers and mild winters.

Italy is very rich in art treasures and many of the world's most famous artists and sculptors were Italian, including Leonardo da Vinci, Giotto, Michelangelo, Bellini and Raphael. Florence, Venice and Rome are the most important cultural centers. Every year fourteen million tourists visit Italy, not only attracted by its culture but also to enjoy the sunshine, the company of warm-hearted and friendly people, and the excellent food and wine.

The Regions of Italy

Italian food in history

The basis of the Italian diet today is a mixture of all kinds of ideas passed down the centuries from the Ancient Greeks and Romans as well as from China and other Eastern countries.

The Romans, for instance, were fond of eating small songbirds such as thrushes and blackbirds, and today in parts of the country these are still considered to be a great delicacy. They also used spices as well as honey, vinegar and wine, in their cooking. Since there were no refrigerators, meat and other foods had to be prepared with large amounts of salt. The flavorings were then added to disguise the saltiness, and the taste of bad meat! *Agrodolce* (sweet and sour) sauces are still popular today.

After Roman times it was not until the sixteenth century that anyone showed much interest in food. Then the powerful Italian

The Doges' Palace in Venice was the scene of lavish banquets.

Fishing is an important industry, especially in Sicily and Sardinia.

families and the Doges (rulers) of Venice, all began to give lavish banquets and an enthusiasm for good food spread all over Italy. In 1533 Catherine de Medici of Florence married the Dauphin (the eldest son of the king of France), later Henry II of France. Her cooks passed on many Italian cooking skills and ingredients to the French.

In the Middle Ages spices from the East Indies, southern India and Sri Lanka were transported by land and sea to Venice and Genoa and then to other parts of Europe by rich Venetian merchants.

Pasta is said to have been brought to Italy from China by the explorer and merchant Marco Polo (1254–1324). Today there are more than 500 types of pasta in Italy.

The first wines were probably cultivated in the Middle East but traces of the plant *vitis vinifera*, producing nearly all the wines of the world, have been found in Italy dating back to 8000 B.C. Wine is as important to the Italian as food and is also a major export product.

Although the Mediterranean is less rich in fish than the Atlantic or North Sea, the fishing industry keeps thousands of Italians at work, particularly the islanders of Sicily and Sardinia. Tuna fish is the most important variety. This is caught around Sardinia and Sicily and shipped over to the canning plants in Liguria for processing. Swordfish, oysters, mussels, prawns, shrimp and cuttlefish are caught in shallow waters, and some of these too are canned or frozen.

Agriculture

In the north

Food growing makes an important contribution to Italy's economy, providing a living for 20 percent of the country's total workforce and contributing 12 percent to the gross national product. The north produces more food than the south, even though there is less land available for agriculture.

The Alps are largely uncultivated

Vineyards on the shores of Lake Garda, the largest lake in Italy. Lemons and olives also grow well in this area.

with more than half given over to forest and 44 percent to pasture. Only 6 percent is cultivated farmland.

On the lower Alpine slopes are vineyards, and small farms producing hay, rye and potatoes. Stone fruits, apples, pears and vines also grow well on some slopes. On the shores of Lake Garda in the northeast lemons, olive groves and vineyards can be found.

The northern lowlands are a most important food-growing area because the soil is good and the climate warm. Cereals, animal fodder and rice are grown here. Around Vercelli there are vast terraced fields of rice, bordered by screens of poplar, elm and willow trees and dotted with huge grain silos and machinery sheds. Rice was first grown in Italy during the sixteenth century and is now an important export crop. Mulberries, apples, pears, plums, cherries and grapevines grow on the plains of Piedmont.

Lombardy is also a fertile area. One of the most important farm activities here is the production of milk for the manufacture of cheese and butter.

Around the lowlands of the Veneto and Friuli – Venezia Giulia, corn is the most important crop, but wheat, sugar beets, vegetables, fruits and vines can be found here too. Many farms keep livestock and poultry.

The plain of Emilia Romagna is a wedge between the Po River, below Piacenza, in the north and the Apennines in the south. Rice is grown here, along with fruit trees, wheat, corn, and vegetables such as peas, beans, potatoes, onions and tomatoes. Most farms keep cattle and pigs.

Liguria slopes down from high mountains to the sea, so most of the area is permanent pasture or woodland, and field crops are grown in only a very small part. The terraced lower slopes are devoted

Newly harvested sugar beets on a farm in Umbria.

9

to vines, figs, olives, citrus fruit and vegetables.

Umbria grows olives, almonds, figs, stone fruits, mulberries and vines, with wheat, beans, corn, tomatoes, sugar beets and potatoes as the most important field crops.

Tuscany is not a particularly fertile area, but corn and alfalfa are important crops and the olive oil of Lucca is particularly good.

Latium, the area around Rome, is quite poor, even though the city itself is not. Wheat is the main crop, though olives are also grown. On the slopes of the Alban hills, vines grow very freely.

The south, Sicily and Sardinia

The south has more farming land than the north, but on the whole it is much poorer. Even with improved transportation facilities and modern farming methods, the trend is for people to leave the south and head for the prosperous north or abroad. Life on a peasant smallholding in parts of southern Italy can be very hard indeed with

In the warm south, all kinds of fruits and vegetables can be seen in the market.

many families barely producing enough food to feed themselves. Nevertheless the climate is warmer than in the north, and many exotic fruits and vegetables grow here.

Campania, the land north and south of Naples, is very fertile. Black, volcanic earth, rich in minerals and irrigated by many rivers, grows a rich variety of fruit and vegetables including eggplant, sweet peppers, chard, tomatoes and potatoes. Citrus fruits grow on the slopes of Mount Vesuvius, the volcano (now extinct) that erupted and caused the destruction of Pompeii and Herculaneum in A.D. 79.

Although the landscape of Apulia is barren and stony, wheat, olive trees, vines, figs, almonds and carob trees grow here, and the land that cannot be cultivated is given over to pasture for sheep.

Calabria and Basilicata are poor regions but the soil is rich and sweet tomatoes, red pimentos, chillies, eggplant, pine nuts and raisins grow well.

In the Abruzzi large numbers of sheep are moved up to the highlands in the summer from the plains below. It is the milk from these flocks that is used to make *pecorino* cheese.

Large trailer-trucks and vans take the farmers' produce from the south to the north along the *autostrade* (highways) that run the length and breadth of Italy.

Sicily is a subtropical island, and

Lemons grow well on the subtropical island of Sicily.

many exotic vegetables and fruits grow here. The lower slopes of Mount Etna, an active volcano erupting every four to twelve years, are particularly fertile. Life for the farmers here is dangerous but the harvests are so rich that they are willing to take the risk to their lives and property. Mount Etna last erupted in 1978.

Sardinia is mainly given over to pasture for sheep and goats (one-third of Italy's stock of these animals graze on the island), although beans, vines and citrus fruits are grown here along with wheat, corn, alfalfa, rice and sugar beets. Much of Sardinia's produce is shipped over to the mainland for processing and export.

Processing the food

Growing crops, catching fish and keeping cattle and pigs produces food, but not all food is eaten fresh or straight from the fields. Much of it has to be processed before it reaches the stores or is exported to other countries.

The largest food-processing factories are in the northern plains. In Emilia Romagna, around Venice and in Lombardy, huge sugar refineries turn the sugar beet crop into white sugar. Fruit and vegetables are canned here too, and the area also makes liqueurs and candy.

Emilia Romagna is famous for processing pork meats and sausage, and in Gorgonzola, Parma, Lodi, Pavia, Piacenze, Bergamo and Milan cheesemaking is an important industry.

The famous Parma ham, made from the legs of fattened, four-month old pigs is produced in Emilia Romagna, Veneto, Lombardy

Many Italian sausages, like the ones being produced in this factory, are exported.

Olive groves near Arezzo in Tuscany. The olive oil produced in this area is particularly good for cooking.

and Piedmont. The hams are salted with sea salt twice or more in the first few days, left in a salting chamber, then stored for several months. They are then washed in warm water, dried and seasoned for another few months. Altogether it takes ten months to make Parma ham.

Outside the northern plains, Campania in the south is the most important food processing area. In addition to the packing and shipping of fresh fruit and vegetables, factories in Campania produce pasta, preserves and a huge amount of peeled tomatoes and tomato paste which is exported all over the world. Over half of the canned and processed fruit and vegetables produced are exported each year.

Olive oil is made mostly from the olives grown in Apulia, Tuscany and Liguria. The silvery leaves of the olive groves make the mountainsides look very attractive.

Although beer is less popular than wine in Italy, most large, northern cities have a brewery.

Besides the large processing plants, most areas also have their own smaller factories. These are set up to make and pack the local specialities such as *panettone* in Milan, *mozzarella* cheese in Campania and almond confectionery in Sicily.

Stores and markets

In the stores

The Italians are very interested in food. According to some national statistics, they spend 38.8 percent of their income on food, compared with 9.5 percent on clothing and 12.14 percent on transportation. So food shopping is an extremely important business and is taken very seriously.

The storekeepers dress up their stores, making them elegant and inviting. The appearance of the store itself is considered almost as important as the quality of the goods on sale.

Italians love to browse and will spend a long time choosing the food they are going to buy. This is one reason why so many smaller stores in Italy survive the competition of supermarkets – even in the towns. Shoppers can chat with the owner, discuss the food, ask for and receive advice.

There is a wide choice of bread in Italy and shoppers can always buy it freshly baked.

The other reason is that convenience foods are far less popular in Italy than they are in other European countries. The Italians prefer to buy their food fresh, and most shoppers go out every day for meat, salad greens, pasta and bread, which in many places is still baked twice daily in time for breakfast and the evening meal. Shopping is considered to be more of an art than a chore.

The Italian specialty shops are particularly appealing. There are some devoted entirely to selling loose pasta in all different shapes and sizes, fresh and dried; others are decorated with hanging *salami* sausages or piled high with enormous Parmesan and *Gorgonzola*

A store like this will have a large variety of pasta for sale. The pasta can be bought either fresh or dried.

cheeses. Ice cream shops (*gelaterie*) look especially inviting with dozens of different flavors on display.

It was the Venetian traders who brought sugar to Italy and inspired the imaginations of Italian pastry cooks and confectioners. Italian pastry cooks are still famous, and pastries, cakes and candy are very popular in Italy. It is quite common to see office and factory workers lining up at a pastry shop for a bag of macaroons or cookies to eat at lunch time. The town of Parma is particularly well known for its pastry shops.

The markets

Despite the arrival of super-markets, many people still do their shopping twice a day and like to buy fresh food whenever possible. One of the great attractions in Italian towns like Venice, Genoa, Turin, Bologna, Florence and Cagliari (on the island of Sardinia) are the bustling, colorful markets where you can buy fish, hams, *salami*, all kinds of cheeses, fruit and vegetables.

Market vendors lead a hectic life, getting up while everyone else is fast asleep to receive boxes of fruit,

You need to be up at dawn to see the food vendors in Venice unloading the gondolas.

meat and vegetables from the country farmers and fresh fish from the ports. The market at Venice, near to the historic Rialto Bridge, is one of the most exciting markets. There are no roads or cars in Venice, so everything must be transported by boat or *gondola* on an intricate network of canals. To see the market at its best you have to be up very early in the morning. Then you will catch the vendors unloading their goods from the *gondolas*. You will also see piles of fish, some of which you would recognize like sole, bass and shrimp, but others you might not such as *vongole* and *canestrelli* (type of clams).

There are even more unusual fish at the market in Genoa: frogfish, sea-hens, scorpions, sea-snails, sea-strawberries and a hairy mussel called *cozze pelose*. Genoans eat a special fish stew called *burrida*, and *cappon magro*, a mixture of shellfish, fish, vegetables and sauce.

Bologna, in the north of the country, is famous for its *salami*-like sausages, which are made from pork, dried and then hung for sale on the market stalls. *Mortadella*, a sausage with penny-sized blobs of white fat mixed in with pink pork is Bologna's best-known sausage.

Carciofi (globe or leaf artichokes) are very common on the vegetable stands, while *carciofi alla giudea* (Jerusalem artichokes) are a Roman speciality and can be found piled high in the markets there. Dark

Above *The fish market in Venice is probably one of the most famous of its kind in the world and sells every type of seafood imaginable.*

purple *melanzane* (eggplant), and luscious tomatoes, olives and *zucchini* (green squash) are all grown in Italy and can be bought there very cheaply.

Carciofi *(globe artichokes), such as this woman is holding, are a common sight in the markets, especially in Rome.*

A tavola (at table)

Prima colazione (breakfast)

Breakfast is the least important meal of the day to the Italians. They eat a "continental" breakfast, that is coffee, hot chocolate or tea with bread, butter and jam. With minor variations and additions (*croissants* in France, for instance, ham and cheese in Holland), this is the early morning feast of most Europeans.

The British cooked breakfast of sausage, egg, bacon and fried bread, or American and Australian specialities such as waffles, pancakes and hefty steaks are not on the menu, except in the restaurants of hotels catering to a large number of tourists.

Breakfast cereals are becoming more popular in some Italian households, particularly with children, but sweet cereals with dried fruit and nuts, and whole wheat bread are not yet popular.

The most important ingredient in an Italian breakfast is coffee. Few Italians drink instant coffee. Ground coffee and whole beans are cheaper there than in some other countries, and coffee is made fresh every morning in most homes. Coffee is made black and strong (*espresso*) although in the morning it is more usual to drink *caffè latte* (coffee with milk). An office worker might well drop into a café or bar on the way to work and order a *cappuccino*. This is coffee that is made with milk whisked up with hot steam to make a thick, frothy topping. The most common home coffee-maker (which can be bought outside Italy) is a simple two-piece metal apparatus which is put on the stove to boil. Far more exciting though are the hissing, chrome-plated steam *espresso* and *cappuccino* machines found in bars and cafes.

The bread, bought fresh every morning and evening because it contains no preservatives to keep it from going stale, comes in long, crusty loaves, often still warm from the baker's oven.

Inside a typical Italian café.

Italian breakfast

You really need a special electric machine to make *cappuccino* coffee, but it is possible to make something very similar with the help of a hand or electric whisk and a little cream.

You will need:
2 tablespoons ground coffee
1 cup water
½ cup milk
sugar to taste
2 large spoonfuls of whipped cream
a little powdered cocoa
fresh, crusty French or Italian bread
sweet (unsalted) butter
apricot jam

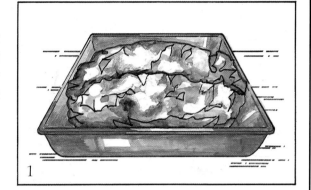

What to do:
Wrap the bread in aluminum foil and put it in a low oven to warm through (1). Put the ground coffee into a jug and pour on very hot, but not boiling, water. Let the coffee grounds settle for a minute or two. Meanwhile heat the milk gently (do not boil or a skin will form). Take the milk from the heat and whisk until very frothy (2). Pour the coffee into cups through a coffee strainer (a fine-meshed tea strainer will do) until the cups are two-thirds full. Pour on the milk, add a small spoonful of whipped cream to each cup (getting it to float on top if possible!) and sprinkle with powdered cocoa (3). This should be enough for two good-sized cups. Take the bread out of the oven, cut into chunks and serve with unsalted butter and apricot jam (4).

Colazione (The midday meal)

Lunch is the most important meal of the day. Offices usually close from noon or 12:30 p.m. until 3 p.m. to allow plenty of time for people to go home for lunch and have a siesta afterward. Although some schools have good cafeterias, many schoolchildren come home for lunch too, so that the meal is often a family affair. Some larger factories and offices have cafeterias too, and sometimes a worker's family can also eat there.

The pasta – spaghetti, *tagliatelli*, ravioli, etc. – soup or, in the north, *risotto* (a rice dish) is eaten first (although in a restaurant an *hors d'oeuvre* may be served before-hand). This is accompanied by crusty bread cut from long, thin loaves. After that comes grilled or sautéed beef or veal with a simple green or tomato salad, well dressed with olive oil, vinegar or lemon, salt and pepper. A bottle of wine and a jug of water are always on the table.

After the meat course, most families will simply have fruit, although cheese and dessert may be eaten in restaurants.

Lunch, which usually consists of several courses, is a time when the whole family gets together. The pasta course, which the family in this picture is about to eat, will generally be followed by a meat course with a salad or vegetables.

Minestrone
Vegetable soup

(There are hundreds of versions of this filling soup – you can really put in any combination of vegetables you like.)

You will need:

4 oz dried white or great northern
   beans
2 carrots
2 small potatoes
1 small turnip
2 onions
1 stalk of celery
4 tomatoes or a tablespoon of tomato
   paste
½ small cabbage
2 slices of bacon
2 oz any small pasta shapes
   (eg little stars or shells)
2 cloves of garlic
1 tablespoon mixed herbs
salt and pepper
2 tablespoons olive oil
Parmesan cheese

What to do:

Soak the dried beans in cold water overnight. Next day peel the potatoes and turnip, skin the tomatoes, scrape the carrots and chop all the vegetables (1). Fry the onion and garlic in the oil along with the chopped bacon and herbs (2). Add the chopped tomatoes and let the mixture simmer a little. Drain the beans and add the tomato mixture and 2 quarts of hot water. Simmer gently for 2 hours. Now add the carrots and after 15 minutes the turnips and potatoes (3). A few minutes before serving add the celery, the cabbage cut in strips and the pasta. Add salt to taste and pepper and a couple of tablespoons of grated Parmesan cheese (4).

Out for dinner

Although Italy is not a rich country, the people enjoy eating out, whether it is a matter of a quick bowl of spaghetti or a celebratory feast. On special occasions the whole family including cousins, aunts and grandparents will go out to a restaurant.

One of the most popular types of restaurants is the *pizzeria*. The pizza (which just means "pie") and the *pizzeria* were invented by the Neapolitans, although now pizzas can be eaten all over Italy and abroad. But pizzas cooked in Italian ovens with home-grown flour and olive oil always seem to taste better than the ones served in other countries. It's not too difficult to make pizzas at home (see recipe below) and you can top them with all kinds of things such as ham,

In pizzerias like the one in this picture, you can sit at your table and watch your pizza being made and cooked in the huge clay ovens.

salami, mushrooms, sweet corn and peppers.

Other restaurants (*trattorie* or *ristorante*) offer a first course followed by a pasta dish, then a main dish and then a dessert and, sometimes, cheese. A restaurant will usually offer a house or local wine which is considerably cheaper than others on the wine list.

In cities and other places that entertain a large number of foreign visitors each year, the restaurants often offer a *menu turistico* (tourist menu) with an all-inclusive price.

Tourist menu

Pasta in brodo (clear soup with little pieces of pasta floating in it)

Prosciutto e melone (melon with thin sliced, cured ham)

Spaghetti alle vongole (spaghetti with clam sauce)

Risotto alla milanese (Milanese style rice)

Vitello al limone (veal with lemon sauce)

Petti di pollo e patate fritte (little pieces of fried chicken and chips)

Fritto misto di mare (mixed fried seafood)

Insalata verde (green salad)

Gelato (ice cream)

Formaggio (cheese)

Caffè (coffee)

Pizza Napoletana
Neapolitan pizza

You will need:

1 cup unbleached flour
¼ oz (1 package) dry yeast
a little warm water
4 or 5 fresh or canned tomatoes
6 anchovy fillets from a can or jar
oregano or basil (herbs)
3 oz *mozzarella* cheese, (or *Bel Paese* or *gruyère*) grated
olive oil
a few black olives

What to do:

Dissolve the yeast in water according to instructions on the package. Pour the flour onto a pastry board, make a well in the center and pour in the yeast mixture (1). Add a little salt. Blend the flour and yeast and add enough water to make a stiff dough (about ¼ cup). Knead the dough until it feels light and elastic, then roll it into a ball and put it on a floured plate. Cover with a clean cloth and let it rise in a warm place like a warming oven. In about 2 hours it should have doubled in size. Now roll out the dough into a large disc about 0.5 cm (¼ in) thick (2). Skin and chop the tomatoes (canned tomatoes will not need to be skinned), and grate the cheese (3). Spread the tomatoes on top of the pizza, season with salt and pepper, arrange the anchovy fillets on top and then add the grated cheese. Sprinkle on oregano or basil, and pour a little olive oil on top.

Add a little more oil to a large baking dish, put in the pizza and cook in a hot oven for about 20–30 minutes. You can add a few black olives before serving if you like (4).

Café life

Italy is a nation of coffee drinkers and most people of all ages pop into a bar at least once a day for a quick *cappuccino* or *espresso*.

Cafés serve alcohol too. They are open all day and all evening and, unlike American bars, they welcome children. Vermouth, *grappa*, red wine and beer are all favorite drinks for an Italian. The children drink *aranciata* (orangeade) or *una Coca* (Coca Cola).

Many cafés also sell food – pizzas with dozens of different toppings, pasta dishes, sandwiches, little cakes, a variety of ice creams – and are very popular with anyone wanting a quick snack during the day. In the evening cafés are convenient places to meet friends.

Many Italian cafés have tables outside. Sitting in a quiet square or a busy street with a *gelato* (ice cream) and watching the world go by is a popular pastime for tourists

Like most cafés, this café in Verona serves alcoholic drinks as well as espresso, caffè latte *and* cappuccino.

and Italians alike. However, in the big cities it is more expensive to sit down outside a café than it is to stand up at the bar inside and it is usually only the tourists or rich businessmen who are willing to spend the extra money for the pleasure of a drink in the sun.

There are some very famous cafés with good reputations and expensive prices. "Florians," in St. Mark's Square in Venice, is one of the best-known cafés in Italy. It was founded in 1720 and in earlier days was the favorite meeting place of such famous figures as Lord Byron the poet, Wagner the composer and the writer George Sand. It is still fashionable, still patronized by the rich and famous, and inside is very beautifully decorated with mirrors and paintings. In the summer visitors to Venice can sit at the tables outside in the *piazza*, watching the pigeons hovering over St. Mark's and listening to a band playing in the square.

In the big tourist centers like Venice, cafés where the customers can sit outside and enjoy the scenery, always attract the tourists.

National specialities

Ice cream

You might think that no one ate ices until after the refrigerator had been invented, but in fact we know that the Ancient Romans made iced wine and fruit juices and learned how to preserve ice in summer. Ices have been popular in Italy ever since, and Italian recipes are enjoyed in other countries too.

In 1533 Catherine de Medici went to France to marry the Dauphin. She took with her a Florentine cook called Buontalenti, who introduced water ices (or *sorbets*) to the French

Ice cream shops, or gelaterie, *serve many different flavored ices.*

court. It is also said that another Italian, de Mirra, brought water ices to the English court of Charles I.

In 1670 a Sicilian, Francisco Procopio, opened the first café in Paris for the sale of ices. Before long, similar establishments were set up all over the city. However, it was not until the second half of the eighteenth century that another famous Italian café owner, Tortoni, invented ice cream, made with fresh cream rather than with water.

Giovanni Bosio, from Genoa, was the first person to sell ice cream in America. Now, of course, Americans have many delicious ice cream recipes.

Most ices and ice creams sold in

Italy today are mass-produced, but if you want to enjoy a real treat it's worth looking for those cafés that do still make their own.

There are several different types of Italian ice on sale in Italy and abroad. *Granita* is a water ice that is made with water, sugar and flavoring. Most refreshing is *granita di limone* (lemon water ice).

Gelato is ice cream, which is best made using fresh cream and sometimes eggs (see the recipe for *gelato di fragole*, strawberry ice cream, given below.) *Cassata* is a mixture of ice cream and candied fruit and *semifreddo* is a mixture of cake, ice cream and fruit.

Gelato di fragole
Strawberry ice cream

You will need:
1 qt fresh strawberries
½ pint heavy cream
½ cup sugar

What to do:
Pulp the strawberries by cooking gently until they are soft and forcing the fruit through a sieve into a bowl (1). In another bowl, whip the cream with the sugar until it is thick (2). Add the strawberry pulp (3), put the mixture into an ice tray and cover with aluminum foil. Freeze for 2 to 2½ hours, stirring thoroughly after the first hour (4). When served, this ice cream should be thick and creamy, not like a block of ice.

Wines and other drinks

The ancient Cretans called Italy "Enotria," the land of wine, still a suitable description today. Italy is one of the world's largest wine producers and, as you can see from the map of the growing areas, there is hardly any part of the country where grapevines are not cultivated and wine is not produced. The best wines come from the northern regions, especially Tuscany, Lombardy, Piedmont and the Veneto.

There are over 1,000 varieties of the plant *vitis vinifera*, the wine-producing grapes, in Italy, and in the different regions there is a huge variation in the way the vines are planted, trained and pruned.

Winegrowers range from the small peasant farmer producing, by primitive, age-old methods, just enough wine for his family and perhaps to supply the local bar, to the huge international wine companies bottling famous wines such as *Soave*, *Lambrusco* and *Valpolicella*.

However large or small the grower, the vines have to be looked after very carefully during the year to make sure the weather or pests do not ruin the grapes. When the grapes are ripe they must be harvested (in September and October) and allowed to ferment with sugar and yeast (which turns the grape juice into alcohol). Then the wine is put in casks to mature before it is finally bottled. Some of the better wines for export are labeled with the initials

Tuscany is one of the largest wine-producing areas. Grapes from these vines will be made into Chianti.

28

1 Dolcetto
2 Gavi
3 Bardolino
4 Valpolicella
5 Soave
6 Asti Spumanti
7 Barbaresco
8 Barolo
9 Lambrusco
10 Chianti
11 Chianti Classico
12 Frascati
13 Verdicchio
14 Corvo
15 Marsala

Map showing where the internationally famous wines originate.

DOC (*Denominazione di Origine Controllata*). These wines have satisfied strict government quality requirements.

Italy also makes vermouth, a sweet or dry aperitif based on a blend of wines flavored with herbs, which is very important for export, and Sicily produces *Marsala*, a sweet, fortified wine invented by two Englishmen, John and William Woodhouse, when they were visiting Sicily in 1760. *Marsala* was a favorite drink of Lord Nelson, the British hero of the Battle of Trafalgar (1805).

Other special Italian drinks include *grappa*, a very strong "firewater" made from compressed grape skins, pits and stems left over after wine making; *strega* (literally meaning "witch") is a sweetish herbal drink and is said to have been first produced by a coven of witches, which met by the banks of the Sabato River in Naples. *Strega* was supposed to be a magic love potion. *Galliano*, named for Giuseppe Galliano, a heroic nineteenth-century Italian major, is a sweet, bright yellow, herbal drink extremely popular in the United States. It is an important ingredient in the cocktail known as a "Harvey Wallbanger" (orange juice, vodka and *galliano*).

Apart from Coca Cola, *limonata* and *aranciata* (lemonsoda and orangeade), the most delicious nonalcoholic drink in Italy is lemonade made from the juice of freshly squeezed lemons, mixed with sugar and water.

Most areas produce and bottle their own wine. Many can be bought in the United States.

Cheeses

Some of the most famous cheeses in the world are produced in Italy.

Parmigiano-reggiano (Parmesan), also called *grana*, was first produced in the tenth or eleventh century on either side of the Po River. Today about 2,300 dairy farms around Parma, Piacenza, Ferrara and Bologna process 700,000 tons of milk a year for the production of this cheese, which is used as a seasoning on pasta and rice dishes. The cheese takes one and a half to

Italy produces a variety of different cheeses, many of which are now popular abroad.

two years to ripen and keeps at room temperature for two to three months. It is an important export cheese, but whereas abroad it is most commonly found already grated in sealed containers, in Italy each household keeps a block of rock-hard *grana* in the larder so that it can be grated freshly every day.

Gorgonzola, a strong-tasting, blue-veined soft cheese is named after a town 19 km (12 miles) from Milan, at the bottom of the first slopes of the Alps. It is said that it was first made 100 years ago by shepherds taking their flocks of sheep from the Alpine pastures down to the plains and stopping in Gorgonzola to rest. Today it is manufactured mostly in small dairies in the Po plains, although some larger plants do exist. It is left to turn blue naturally, a process that is speeded up by putting copper wires through the cheese. *Gorgonzola* has been an important export cheese since 1870.

Mozzarella is a sweetish cheese which is delicious eaten on its own with bread when it is fresh but is also used for the cheesy topping on pizzas. In the past it was produced in southern Italy almost entirely from buffalo milk, and was considered a great delicacy, but now it is made in the north as well, particularly in Lombardy, and cow's milk is usually used.

Ricotta is made from the whey of *mozzarella*, *provolone* and other cheeses, so it is really a "twice-

Mozzarella is delicious eaten raw, or used for pizza topping.

cooked" cheese. It is soft and mild and used a great deal for desserts and flavorful cakes.

Pecorino romano is a cheese with a long history. It is described in the *De Rustica* of Lucius Junius Moderatus Columella, who in the first century B.C. stopped in Rome having reached Italy with Hannibal's armies. *Pecorino romano* is a popular cheese abroad, particularly in the United States, the home of a great number of immigrant Italians. Other delicious cheeses to look for are *taleggio, fontina, caciocavallo, Bel Paese, dolcelatte* and *fiore sardo*.

Pasta

There are over 500 varieties of pasta (or *pasta asciutta* to give it its full name) in Italy, and nearly every region has its own speciality and delicious sauce. For instance, the Venetians make a sweet pasta dish with cinnamon and sugar; in the south they use chillies in a hot sauce that burns your tongue if you are not used to it; in Lombardy melted cheese and onions are popular sauces with pasta dishes.

In Italy today, pasta is a very important part of the diet. It is still made daily in many homes there, but these days it is also made in huge pasta factories, which sprung up all over the country in the late nineteenth century.

Although it is often said that pasta was introduced into Italy from the far east by the explorer and merchant, Marco Polo, Etruscan frescoes found in Tuscany show that a type of pasta was made in these ancient times, and the Greeks and Romans also included pasta in their diet. Historical evidence shows too that Arab invaders introduced spaghetti into Sicily long before Marco Polo's day.

In the eighteenth century, it was

Pasta comes in many different shapes, sizes and colors.

fashionable for young, rich Englishmen to make a grand tour of Europe. One group came back from Italy and started the "Macaroni Club" in London. Here they served pasta to other young men, who became known as "Macaronis." As well as enjoying platefuls of pasta, they also wore special clothes: exaggeratedly tall hats and colorful topcoats.

Pasta can be bought fresh or dried and can be made with all kinds of different flours, depending on the variety. Some pasta contains egg, and some is made with spinach which turns it green. Some – such as ravioli and *tortellini* – are stuffed with cheese, meat or vegetables. Popular types of pasta include *tagliatelle*, *penne*, *vermicelli*, *orecchiette*, *linguine*, and *rigatoni*.

Rigatoni con la ricotta
Short pasta with soft cheese

This is a bit like a custard and is served in Rome as a dessert.

You will need:
7 oz of small *rigatoni* or macaroni
3½ oz *ricotta* or cottage cheese
2 heaping teaspoons sugar
¼ teaspoon ground cinnamon
a little warm milk

What to do:
Cook the pasta in plenty of boiling, salted water until just tender (about 6–8 minutes) (1). Meanwhile cream the ricotta with the sugar and cinnamon, adding enough of the warm milk to make a smooth sauce (2). Drain the pasta and stir in the cheese mixture (3). You can sprinkle some more cinnamon on top if you wish.

Safety note: Get an adult to drain the pasta. Boiling water burns!

Regional specialities

The north

There are no general northern Italian dishes – each area has its own specialities.

In the Veneto, (Venice and the surrounding areas), *polenta* is a speciality. This is a kind of pudding made with cornmeal. It can be boiled, fried, toasted, baked with meat or tomato sauce or served with butter and cheese. Venice is also famous for *bigoli*, a kind of strong-tasting spaghetti, made of whole wheat and the dishes *risi e bisi* (*risotto* with peas) and *fegato alla veneziana* (calves' liver cooked in butter and onions).

In Tuscany, (the region surrounding Florence), steaks washed down with *Chianti Classico*, the most famous Italian wine of all, are very popular. *Pecorino* cheese is used a good deal in cooking, and so are local olive oil and herbs. *Pappardelle con la lepre* is a kind of pasta with hare sauce.

Emilia Romagna (which includes Bologna) is famous for *Bolognese*

Ciambella *cakes are popular in the north, as well as other parts of the country.*

Tagliatelle alla Bolognese
Tagliatelle with Bolognese sauce

You will need:

18 2 oz *tagliatelle*
½ oz chopped mushrooms (optional)
4 tablespoons (½ stick) butter or
    margarine
2 slices bacon, chopped
1 stalk celery, chopped
1 large carrot, chopped
1 small onion, chopped
¾ lb lean chopped beef
2 teaspoons tomato paste
1 cup of stock, made with a beef
    bouillon cube and boiling water
about ½ cup milk
grated Parmesan cheese

What to do:

Melt the butter in a casserole and fry the bacon in it for a minute or two. Add the celery, carrot, mushrooms and onion and soften before adding the beef and browning it (1). Pour on half the stock and let the mixture bubble until the liquid is absorbed. Add salt and pepper and stir. Now add the tomato paste and the rest of the stock. Cover and cook very slowly for 1½ hours, stirring occasionally and adding more stock if the sauce gets too dry (2). Add the milk toward the end of the cooking time (3).

Boil a large pot of salted water and cook the *tagliatelle*. Pile on a warm dish and top with the sauce. Pass the Parmesan at the table (4). Serves 4–6.

Safety note: Beware of sharp knives. Ask an adult to help you chop vegetables.

sauce, usually served with *tagliatelle* (⅛-in-wide strips of pasta). Other specialities include *mortadella* (see page 16).

Liguria is probably most famous for the Genoese *pesto*, a green sauce for pasta made from basil, oil and garlic.

In Piedmont (which borders France, and includes the city of Turin and the Aosta valley), rice is more popular than pasta. The white truffle, a little greeny-yellow plant that grows under willow, oak and poplar trees, is found here. It is very expensive as it has to be sniffed out by specially trained dogs. Truffles are made into sauces or used for the dish *fagiano al tartufo* (pheasant stuffed with truffles).

Lombardy is famous for *minestrone*, *osso buco* (veal bones cooked in a sauce) and *panettone*, (a very light Italian version of Christmas fruit cake). *Cotoletta milanese* (veal cutlets rolled in breadcrumbs and egg and fried in butter) is a speciality of Milan. *Gorgonzola* and *Bel Paese* cheeses are also made in this area.

The main dishes of The Marches on the Adriatic coast, are spit roasts, fish soups and *vincisgrassi* (a regional version of *lasagne*).

Umbria is the home of black truffles, and *spaghetti al tartufi* (spaghetti with truffles) is a well known dish.

In Latium, the region around Rome, pasta sauces are strong-tasting and rich – made from chicken livers, hams, bacon, eggs, meat and chicken – and are served with *fettucini*, the ribbon-shaped Roman version of *tagliatelle*. Romans also enjoy *zuppa di pesce* (fish soup) and exotic vegetables such as *carciofi* (globe artichokes) and *asparagi di campo* (wild asparagus), which grows in the surrounding countryside.

The south

Although the south is on the whole not as wealthy as the industrial north, there is nothing poor about the food to be found there.

In Abruzzi and Molise, one of the famous dishes is *maccheroni alla chitarra* (macaroni guitar style), so-called because the pasta is cut on a special wood and wire contraption that looks like a guitar. This is eaten with *pecorino* cheese and tomatoes. Here too you can eat *minestrone delle virtu* (a thick soup containing just about every type of vegetable grown in the region along with strips of meat and pasta). Grilled trout, stuffed cuttlefish and sole with black olives are seafood specialities found on the coast.

Campania is the region that includes Naples, where pizza was first invented. Naples is also famous for its *pizzaiola* (tomato and garlic) sauce for pasta and meat. *Sfogliatelle* (sweet *ricotta* cheese turnovers), and eggplant *alla parmigiana* (with Parmesan cheese) are other popular dishes.

Locally caught swordfish is especially popular in Sicily.

Roasting on a spit, grilling over hot coals and frying are the most common ways of cooking in Apulia, which is partly influenced by Ancient Greek, Arabian and Neapolitan customs. Endive, asparagus, fennel and artichokes are some of the vegetables grown. *Orecchiette* ("little ears," so called because of the shape) is a famous local pasta. It is made from semolina (durum wheat flour).

Calabria, at the "toe" of Italy, and Basilcata are poor regions. In the past Calabria was once colonized by Ancient Greeks and Romans, and there is also evidence of Byzantine and Arabic civilization. All these settlers have influenced cooking methods so the food varies enormously from one part of the region to another. In rural areas, meat and pasta are flavored strongly with hot peppers and chillies (you can see strings of peppers hung out to dry on balconies throughout the region); in the mountains fresh forest herbs are used to flavor game meat, trout and mushrooms; on the coast tuna and swordfish cooked with capers and olives, and sardines flavored with the herb oregano are favorites. Other main dishes include *spaghetti con broccoli* (spaghetti with broccoli), *sagne chine* (lasagne with artichokes and meatballs), *cannariculi* (fritters with honey) and *alici al limone* (fresh anchovies baked with lemon juice).

Sardinia

Sardinia is the second largest Italian island after Sicily. It is rocky and barren-looking, but beautiful with silvery granite mountains, dark woods perfumed with myrtle trees, a wild coastline and a very blue sea.

The Sardinians eat a lot of roast lamb, kid and pork: *porchetta*, tender young roast piglet-on-a-spit, is a very popular dish. Another speciality is *trattalia* made of lamb entrails.

The game is good too. Wild boar, venison, rabbit, snipe and quail are all to be found on the island. On the

Spaghetti con broccoli
spaghetti with broccoli
(Calabria)

You will need:
1 lb 5 oz spaghetti
2 lb broccoli (fresh or frozen)
2 cloves crushed garlic
6 tablespoons olive oil
1¾ lb fresh tomatoes, skinned and
  chopped
3 oz raisins
2 tablespoons chopped parsley
1 oz mixed chopped nuts

What to do:
Wash the broccoli in salted water, and break up into small florets. (Frozen broccoli can be cooked straight from the package.) Boil a large pot of salted water for the pasta, and another smaller one for the broccoli (1). Fry the garlic in the oil until golden, add the tomatoes and cook gently for 10 minutes (2). Add the nuts and raisins, and let this simmer while you cook the broccoli and the pasta, until both are just tender (about 10 minutes each) (3). Drain both. Put the pasta in a warm bowl, top with the broccoli and then pour the sauce on top. Sprinkle with parsley before serving (4). Serves a hungry family of 5 or 6.

Safety note:
Peel the tomatoes by letting them sit in just-boiled water for about one minute: boil a pot of water, turn off the heat, and then put the tomatoes in. Ask an adult to help you.

market stands thrushes, blackbirds and other small birds are piled high waiting to be sold. *Taccula* is a dish of thrush roasted in myrtle leaves.

The fish in Sardinia is delicious: tuna and white bream from the Mediterranean and river fish such as trout are all popular, and the lobster, served in soups and stews and grilled is famous.

Sardinian cheeses such as *raviggiolu* made from goat's milk, *cacio fiore* and *ricotta* are also delicious.

Sicily

Many of the most famous Italian specialities come from Sicily, a luxuriant, fertile island, quite different from the wilder-looking

Taccula *is as popular in Sardinia today as it was in Roman times.*

Sardinia. The fruit, vegetables, cereals and olives grown here are some of the best in Europe.

The fish is excellent around these waters. *Pasta con le sarde* (pasta with sardines) and *pescespada* (swordfish stuffed with brandy, *mozzarella* cheese and herbs and grilled on charcoal) are dishes well worth trying. Sea bass, lobster, prawns, giant mullet and swordfish cooked with capers, raisins, pine nuts and olives are other specialities.

The Sicilians love sweets and desserts. *Frutti di marturana* are brightly colored, realistic-looking fruits made of marzipan. Other confectionery is made with almonds, candied lemon peel and honey. Prickly pears, quince and *cassata* (a variety of ice cream containing candied fruit) are popular desserts. Most Italians think that Sicilian ice cream

is the best in the world.

Marsala is a fortified wine (see page 29) made on the island, and there is a great variety of liqueurs and bitters made locally with lemons, herbs and almonds.

Arance caramellizzate
Caramel oranges (Sicily)

You will need:
4 oranges
peel of two more oranges
1 cup of sugar
1 cup of water

What to do:
Peel four oranges very carefully with a sharp knife, getting rid of all the pith (1). Make a syrup by heating the sugar and water gently on the stove. When it is thick, dip the oranges into the syrup, turning them over so that the whole orange is well coated (2). This should take only 2 or 3 minutes. Take out the oranges and arrange them on a large dish. Now cut the peel from two other oranges very thin (use a potato peeler). Cut this into fine matchstick shapes (3). Plunge them into boiling water and cook for a few minutes to get rid of the bitter taste. Drain, then heat in the syrup until the strips begin to look transparent. Add a tablespoon of the syrup mixture to the top of each orange and chill the oranges until they are very cold (4). Serves 4.

Safety note: Ask an adult to help you peel the oranges, dip them in the syrup, and boil and drain the orange peel.

Festive foods

Italians enjoy celebrating, and parties, feasts and holidays are times to be enjoyed by all the family. As it is a Catholic country, there are several saints days in the year and it is customary for sincere

Weddings, such as this one in Calabria, are times of celebration and feasting.

prayer to go hand in hand with good food and drink.

Italians do not have the heavy, fruity variety of Christmas pudding and fruit cake but they have their own version, which comes from Milan. This is called *panettone*, a kind of light sponge dotted with raisins. *Panettone* comes in all sizes, is packed in blue boxes and is a traditional Christmas gift.

Pinoccate are macaroons made with pine nuts, a Perugian speciality for Christmas and the feast of the Epiphany on January 6. *Colomba* (literally meaning "dove") is an Easter cake from Milan. Other special Easter foods include the Genoese *torta pasqualina* (Easter cake) and *pasticceria napoletana*, a very rich and elaborately decorated cake found in Naples.

Easter Sunday in Rome is a happy religious occasion. Every year thousands of Catholics from all over the world gather in St. Peter's Square on that special holy day to receive the Pope's blessing. The stores are all brightly decorated, selling souvenirs and traditional, prettily decorated little Easter cakes.

Torrone, or nougat, is a traditional candy for holy days, although some saints are associated with particular food. For instance *zeppole di San Giuseppe* are ring doughnuts made especially for Saint Joseph's day (March 19) and are sold at street stands set up for the occasion.

If candy and cake are traditional festive food, so too are elaborate roasts. It is difficult to imagine anything more elaborate than the Sardinian *malloru de su sabatteri* (cobbler's bull), so called because the meat to be roasted is literally sewn together before it is cooked. It is made of animals stuffed with other animals, each smaller than the last. So a hare will be stuffed into a suckling pig which will be sewn into a goat and the whole thing sewn into a calf. Or a turkey will contain a duck, a snipe and a thrush. This is then cooked for several hours *a carrargiu*, that is, in a ditch dug out of the ground in the open air and covered with olive and myrtle branches to flavor the meat. This is a traditional Sardinian method of roasting and has remained unchanged for hundreds of years.

A parade in Sardinia. Festivals are occasions for dressing up and traditional food which, in Sardinia, includes malloru de su sabatteri.

Italian food in other countries

There are few big cities in Europe, North America or Australia that do not have at least one Italian restaurant. From the cheaper pizzerias to the very elegant and expensive restaurants, Italian food has become very popular abroad.

The main reason for this is the large numbers of Italians who have, since the late nineteenth century, emigrated out of Italy. During economically troubled times up until World War I, and again after World War II, when poverty and unemployment swept the country, it became the policy of the Italian government to encourage emigration to more prosperous parts of the world. Many factory workers, tailors and café and restaurant owners left their homeland and started their businesses in other countries. There is a big Italian population in America, Canada and Australia, with France, Belgium, West Germany and Britain having also provided a new homeland for

These days, Italian cafés and restaurants can be found all over the world. This one is in London.

Italian immigrants.

The most common Italian restaurant outside of Italy is the *pizzeria* offering an alternative to the American hamburger and fried chicken varieties of fast food.

Simple Italian restaurants serving all kinds of pasta plus a few basic veal and chicken dishes are also popular. The food offered in these cheaper restaurants, however, is adapted to suit the local population and is not truly Italian. In an inexpensive Italian restaurant in the United States, although the waiters might be natives of Naples, the food will be "Americanized." Veal, for example will come with potatoes and beans, rather than with a simple green salad and the pasta will usually be offered with only one or two sauces, *Napoletana* (tomato and garlic) or *Bolognese* (meat and tomato). Both tend to lack the authentic rustic Italian taste. It is necessary to eat at an expensive restaurant – more expensive than a similar establishment in Italy – before you get the real thing and a decent choice of Italian dishes.

In addition to starting up restaurants, Italian immigrants in various countries have also been responsible for creating a demand for certain Italian specialties to be imported. This fact has improved Italian export figures for such foods as cheeses, pasta and *panettone*.

Italian wines are also popular abroad, although most experts

The Italian sector of New York is known as "Little Italy."

agree that the quality is less good than French wines. The most popular can be found on the wine lists of most liquor stores and Italian restaurants. In some places abroad, specialist Italian wine shops are geared to improving the public's knowledge of Italian wine. In London, the "Enoteca" (literally "repository of wines"), stocks thousands of different varieties from the nineteen wine-growing regions of Italy. The Enoteca also organizes study seminars and talks for students of the wine trade, wine societies and the general public, and has leaflets available on Italian wines.

Glossary

Brewery A factory where beer is made.

Chard (also called Swiss chard) The greens of a type of beet, with large leaves and thick stalks.

Confectioners Candy makers.

Convenience foods Canned or frozen foods which require very little preparation at home.

Economic European Community (EEC) A group of European countries formed on January 1, 1958, for the purpose of making special arrangements for buying and selling each others' products, making laws and deciding other important matters that affect each member country.

Ferment To cause a change in a substance by adding something (such as yeast) which produces chemical changes.

Fertile Producing much fruit or large crops, as in "fertile soil."

Fortified wine Wine which has had alcohol added, either to improve or preserve it.

Frescoes Paintings made on walls freshly covered with wet plaster.

Gross national product The total value of all goods and services produced annually by a country.

Gondola A long narrow boat found only in Venice. It is steered by a *gondolier* who stands in the back and poles the *gondola* along with a long oar.

Hors d'oeuvre An appetizer served before a meal.

Immigrant A person who permanently moves from his or her home country to another.

Pasture Grassy land where cattle and sheep graze.

Peninsula A long narrow piece of land jutting out into the sea.

Plain A flat area of land where it is often easy to grow crops.

Republic A country ruled by a president, not by a king or queen.

Semolina The hard grains, usually of wheat, left over after milling. Often used in Italian puddings and pasta.

Suckling pig A young pig that is still taking milk from its mother.

Italian words and phrases

General

Buongiorno	Good morning
Buona notte	Good night
Per favore	Please
Ciao	Hi, hello, goodbye
Arrivederci	Goodbye (more formal than *ciao*)
Vorrei	I would like
Dov'è . . . ?	Where is . . . ?

Che orè sono, per favore?
What time is it, please?

Come si chiama?
What is your name?

Mi chiamo Anna.
My name is Anna.

Mi piace molto l'Italia.
I like Italy very much.

Abito a Londra/Parigi/Sydney
I live in London/Paris/Sydney.

Food

Il pane	Bread
Il burro	Butter
Il formaggio	Cheese
Il pomodoro	Tomato
Il pesce	Fish
La carne	Meat
Il pollo	Chicken
Le patate	Potatoes
Il vitello	Veal
La bistecca	Beef steak
Il vino	Wine
La pesca	Peach
Una limonata	A glass of lemonade

At the restaurant

Vorrei una tavola per tre persone per l'una, per favore.
I would like a table for three people for one o'clock, please.

Ho fame.
I am hungry.

Ho sete.
I am thirsty.

Vorrei una bistecca a la napoletana/ fritto misto di mare, per favore.
I would like a steak with Neopolitan sauce/mixed fried fish, please.

Il conto, per favore.
The bill, please.

Posso avere un bicchiere/coltello/ forchetta, per favore?
Could I have a glass/knife/fork, please.

Una bottiglia di vino rosso/acqua minerale, per favore.
A bottle of red wine/mineral water, please.

Books to read

Birch, Beverly. *Lets Look Up Food from Many Lands.* Morristown, NJ: Silver Burdett, 1985.

Bisignano, Alphonse. *Cooking the Italian Way.* Minneapolis, MN: Lerner Publications, 1982.

Deming, Mary and Joyce Haddard. *Follow the Sun: International Cookbook for Young People.* Danbury, CT: Sun Scope Publishing, 1982.

Grossman, Ronald. *Italians in America,* revised edition. Minneapolis, MN: Lerner Publications, 1979.

Leech, Michael. *Italy.* Morristown, NJ: Silver Burdett, 1976.

Stein, R. *Italy.* Chicago, IL: Childrens Press, 1983.

Time-Life Books, ed. *Fresh Ways with Pasta.* Morristown, NJ: Silver Burdett, 1986.

Time-Life Publishers. *Italian Menus.* Morristown, NJ: Silver Burdett, 1985.

Picture acknowledgments

The publishers would like to thank the following for their permission to reproduce copyright pictures: Anthony Blake cover, 12, 13, 17 (top), 30, 31 (bottom) 38, 40 The J. Allen Cash Photolibrary 41 Hutchinson Library 10, 24, 36, 42, 43 John Topham Picture Library 11, 25, 33 Wayland Picture Library 9, 18, 20, 22 George Wright 14, 15, 26, ZEFA 6, 7, 8, 16, 17 (bottom), 28, 29, 31 (top), The maps on pages 5 and 29 are by Malcolm Walker. The recipe illustrations are by Juliette Nicholson.

Index